AF399443

# *Winter is coming*

## *International Poetry*


*Edited by*
# *Gino Leineweber*


*Verlag Expeditionen*

Publisher: Verlag Expeditionen, 2020
Winter is Coming
International Poems
Edited by Gino Leineweber

Cover Photo: Jill Wellington, Pixabay License
Cover Design: Birgitta Sjöblom

ISBN 978-3-947911-27-1

To appreciate the beauty of a snowflake
it is necessary to stand out in the cold
*Aristotle*

# TABLE OF CONTENTS

# THE SNOW
*Ahmet Özer, Turkey*


sniffing a rhythmical air the snow falls
on all the times of the world that witness our lives
on the white page of our voice / on eternity
on the childish loneliness of our flowing days
from the grey sky sparkles pour down on
the locked doors of the dirge behind us.


to the leafless branch of the cherry that misses its
    flower
the wind releases a bird with no direction to fly to
two eyes / a beating heart / the glances flowing off of
    the windows
travel with the trains setting forth for long trips
kissing the face of the earth the snow constantly falls.


sprinkling the magic of joy on dark seas
snow places the sorrow of the evening in our infant
    dreams
brings the years wrapped in silk to our windows
and adds many an embroidery to the songs that raise
    life.
clock sounds / passengers into night / the humming of
    the stations
raise the pages of the diary left half-finished
written on the diary of love whose salt is upon our lips

and leave a drop of blood at the endless page of
   history
the sound that makes the earth think grows: the snow
   falls.

KAR
*Ahmet Özer, Türkiye*


kar yağıyor oynak bir havayı kollayarak
ömrümüze tanık bütün zamanlarına dünyanın
sesimizin bembeyaz sayfasına / sonsuzluğa
akan günlerimizin çocuksu yalnızlığına
gri gökyüzünden ışıltılar sağılıyor
ardımızdaki ağıtın kilitli kapılarına.


çiçeğini özleyen kirazın yapraksız dalına
bir kuşu salıyor rüzgâr uçacağı yön belirsiz
iki göz / çarpan yürek / camlardan akan bakışlar
uzun yolculuğa çıkan trenlere sefer eyliyor
kar aralıksız yağıyor dünyanın yüzünü öperek.


kar sevincin büyüsünü serperek karanlık denizlere
çocuk düşlerimize oturtuyor akşamın hüznünü
ipekle sargılanan yılları getiriyor penceremize
binbir nakış ekliyor yaşamı havalandıran şarkılara.


saatin sesi / geceye giren yolcular / istasyonların
   uğultusu
yarım kalan güncenin sayfalarını havalandırıyor
tuzu dudaklarımızdaki aşkın güncesine yazılan

bir damla kan bırakıyor uçsuz sayfasına tarihin
yeryüzünü düşündüren ses büyüyor: kar yağıyor.

LOSS
*Ali Al-Hazmi, Saudi Arabia*


on the threshold of night
 They await the passing of the last evening
Their eyes filled with sorrow
 They willingly forget themselves in the pathways of
   pains
 Where mistaking them for the flames of estrangement
 from hopes they left behind the path of time,
 you would think they are drunk when they are sober
 But the shock is even harder on a sprout
 in the spring of their eyes
 They did not wish for their wounds to leave their
   footsteps stolen
 at the very start of the path
 where they stayed away from the blossoms of their
   days They rested to an exhausting exile that leafed
   out in
 their chests

 That's how the losers do with their time
 When it is finally time
 When the last path heads nowhere in the face of night
 for they had shared everything
 And no words are left for them from the wine of
 speech to make a judgement
 For so their night didn't care about the screams
 coming from their memories

behind the door of life
Oh, how noble it would have been of their dreams
to stay on paper
in the closet

خُسران
علي الحازمي ، السعودية

على عتبة الليل
ينتظرون مرور المساء الأخير
عيونـهمُ اكتحلت بالأسى
في دروب المواجع ينسون أنفسهم عنوة
حيث تحسبهم من لهيب التغرب
عن أمنياتٍ لهم خلف درب الزمان
سكارى وما هم كذلك
لكن وقع الفجيعة أقسى على برعمٍ
في ربيع عيونـهمُ
لم يشاؤوا على الجرح ترك
خطاهم على أول الدرب مسلوبةً
حيث ظلوا بعيدين عن زهر أيامهم
واستراحوا إلى غربةٍ أورقت
في صدورهمُ بالضنى


هكذا يصنع الخاسرون من العمر
عند انتهاء المطاف بـهم
حيث لا وجهةٌ للممر الأخير أمام المساء
لأنـهم اقتسموا كلَّ شيءٍ
ولم يتبق لهم من نبيذ الكلام كلامٌ
فيحتكمون إليه
لذلك لم يكترث ليلهم بالصراخ
الذي كان يصدر عن ذكريات لهم
خلف باب الحياة
وكم كان أسمى لأحلامهم

أن تظلَّ على ورقٍ
في الخزانة

# VELVET IS NOT FOR THEM
*Annabel Villar, Uruguay/Spain*


Velvet is not for them,
neither lace or muslins,
just rustic clothes,
just rough voices,
just hard gestures.

Books are not for them,
neither desk or academies,
just scrubing/ washing/ stinging/ digging,
planting and harvesting,
dreaming is not allowed

But there is always something worse…

Marginalized behind the veils,
preaching in stony deserts,
in their Third World of camps
without oasis or future or present,
watching  life pass in front of their eyes
narrowed by sun and sadness.

But there is always something worse…

In their patriarchal Third World
of dry woodland ignorance,
marginalized under their tunics
raising children without water but with caltrops,
watching life pass in front of their eyes
clouded by Aids and sorrow.

But there is always something worse…

Marginalized beyond the red slum showcases,
in their unequal and unfair Fourth World
with their noses pressed to the windows,
just watching life pass in front of their eyes
without living it, sidelong, like a spectator.

But there is always something worse…

Among birth and death…
just suspension points.

PARA ELLAS NO SON
LOS TERCIOPELOS
*Annabel Villar, Uruguay/España*


Para ellas no son los terciopelos,
ni los encajes ni las muselinas,
sólo telas rústicas,
sólo voces ásperas,
sólo gestos duros.

Para ellas no son los libros,
ni los pupitres ni las academias,
sólo fregar, lavar, picar, cavar, sembrar y recolectar,
soñar no está permitido.

Pero siempre hay algo peor…

Marginadas tras los velos,
predicando en desiertos pedregosos,
en su tercer mundo de campamentos
sin oasis, ni futuro, ni presente,
viendo pasar la vida ante sus ojos
entrecerrados por el sol y por la pena.

Pero siempre hay algo peor…

Marginadas bajo las túnicas,
criando niños sin agua y con abrojos,
en su tercer mundo patriarcal
y de seca ignorancia selvática,
viendo pasar la vida ante sus ojos
nublados por el sida y por la pena.

Pero siempre hay algo peor…

Marginadas tras los cristales
de los guetos de barrios rojos,
en su cuarto mundo desigual e injusto
de nariz pegada a la ventana,
viendo pasar la vida ante sus ojos,
sin vivirla,
de soslayo,
de prestado.

Pero siempre hay algo peor…

Entre el nacer y el morir…
 sólo ilusorios puntos suspensivos.

# IN THE MIDDLE OF SUMMER
*Anna Nasiłowska, Poland*
*Translated by Joanna Nasiłowska-Rek, Poland*


In winter having once lacked
good shoes
you know
they have to be comfortable
not to slide
not to soak.

In February having once lived
in the attic
where the wind whistles
you appreciate
good windows
and warmth.

During my generation's life
in my homeland
things have changed:
who didn't gather winter supplies
will
go to the supermarket
and buy anything.

But it won't be as good!
Oh, it cannot be compared!

– I'm telling over the cooker
preparing marmalade
stirring sweet fruit pulp
with a ladle.

Such an atavism
in the middle of summer
the breath of frost can be felt
as default.

# W ŚRODKU LATA
*Anna Nasiłowska, Polska*


Kto kiedyś nie miał na zimę
dobrych butów
wie
że muszą być wygodne
nie śliskie
i nieprzemakalne.

Kto choć raz mieszkał w lutym
na poddaszu
gdzie hula wiatr
docenia
dobre okna
i ciepło.

Za życia mojego pokolenia
w moim kraju
zmieniło się:
kto nie zrobił zapasów na zimę
ten
pojedzie do supermarketu
i kupi sobie wszystko.

Ale nie takie!
O, nie ma porównania!
- opowiadam znad garnka
smażąc powidła

mieszając chochą
słodki owocowy miąższ.

Taki atawizm
w środku lata
czuć
domyślny oddech mrozu.

# WINTER SONG
*Anna Würth, Germany*


Your song Lucia
when singing still helped
but then the snow


# SOPHIA
*Anna Würth, Germany*
*Translated by John Waterfield, United Kingdom*

A wind-skewed gait
felt as nettles in the spine
a shock to the vitals
bodily wise
my early warning system ignites
intrinsic physical treasure

WINTERLIED
*Anna Würth, Deutschland*


Dein Lied Lucia
als Singen noch geholfen hat
aber der Schnee


SOPHIA ODER
DIE WEISHEIT DES LEIBES
*Anna Würth, Deutschland*


Ein windschiefer Gang
Nesseln kreuzwärts
der Schlag ins Kontor
körperklug
springt mein Frühwarnsystem an
geschätzte Leibeigenschaft

NEW YEAR'S
*Aristea Papalexandrou, Greece*
*Translated by Philip Ramp, USA/Greece*


Troupes came to us
from abroad
listening to us
left us

Eleven o'clock sleepless
the unlit city heading for
twelve
Vassilopsomo* petrified
calls to mind the unworn silk of a
Jocasta
Happy New Year and Goodnight!

Memories piled in moments
Two thousand and ten…
New year
dawn our diminishing
future.

Mute night.


*Vassilopsomo is a special bread baked in a round loaf for New Year's and is named after St. Basil (Vassily) whose name day is January 1.

ΠΡΩΤΟΧΡΟΝΙΑ
*Αριστέα Παπαλεξάνδρου, Ελλάδα*


Από τα ξένα θίασοι
μας ήρθαν
μας ακούστηκαν
μας φύγαν.

Ώρα ενδεκάτη άγρυπνη
οδεύει το άστυ αφώτιστο στην
δωδεκάτη.
Μαρμαρωμένο βασιλόψωμο
καλεί το αφόρετο μεταξωτό μιας
Ιοκάστης
Καλή χρονιά και Καληνύχτα.

Μνήμες στοιβάζονται στιγμές
Δύο χιλιάδες δέκα…
Νέας χρονιάς
ξημέρωμα το μέλλον
μάς λιγόστεψε.

Νύχτα βουβή.

# THE SKIN OF SNOW IS AN OPEN COVER OF THE DREAM BOX

*Barbara Pogačnik, Slovenia*
*Translated by Jernej Županič, Slovenia*


In the white of the brittle horizon, a rabbit,
white as snow, scurries across the open, past
deadened threads of grass. We walk
with countless steps, weaving our long path
through the shimmer of detached white.
The stalk of sleep breaks among the reeds:
brown peels of letters among sentries of winds.


Books on their shelves have opened onto the field,
the field reads the books and the books read the field.
The room is suspended in the lull.
A coin flies into ringing resolution,
the wheat whispers in the ear but the snow won`t let it
   come forth.
A light-footed figure walks
among the rows of future food, a sentry of winds,
walking lightly, mortally, nigh transformed into wind,
cracking against visions, hollow hazelnuts.


Speech, poured by walking into never,
through the day into droplets of the evening.
Strokes of a swimmer in a sea of nations
that speak and love the word in railroad cars,

strokes – flashes in thin air,
made flesh in the hours of walking through Les
    Fagnes,
in the hours that grow on stalks deep underneath the
    snow
like invisible flowers.

# KOŽA SNEGA JE ODGRNJEN POKROV SANJSKE ŠKATLE

*Barbara Pogačnik, Slovenija*


V belini prhkega obzorja snežno
bel zajec teče po odprtem mimo
omrtvelih travnih nitk. Hodimo
z brezštevilnimi koraki, vijugamo to dolgo pot
med lesketom odmaknjene beline.
Steblo spanca se trga sredi trsja:
rjavi odluščki črk v straži vetrov.


Knjige po policah so se odprle v polje,
polje bere knjige in knjige berejo polje.
Soba visi v brezvetrju.
Kovanec poleti v zvenečo odločilnost,
pšenica zašumi v ušesu, a je sneg ne da.
Med gredice bodoče hrane hodi
postava lahnega koraka, stražnik vetrov,
hodi lahno, smrtno, skoraj spremenjen v veter,
stre se ob privide, prazne lešnike.


Govor, pretočen s hojo v nikoli,
skozi dan v srage večera.
Zamahi plavalca v morju narodov,
ki govorijo in v vagonih ljubijo besedo,
zamahi-bliski v redkem zraku,

potrjeni v urah hoje po Les Fagnes,
v urah, ki pecljate rastejo globoko pod snegom
kot nevidne rože.

BUSINESSMEN
*Barry Stevenson, United Kingdom*


pronounced like firemen, policemen, postmen,
deemed necessary adjunct to a civil society :
one's in building, the other's in the car trade,
both in tee-shirts, shades, bermudas,
posing for a picture.
The smiles look genuine.
The two girls are laughing.
One has his arm round her shoulder,
the other an arm round her waist.
Drinks. A certain panache.
Money's changed hands, a deal's been done.

They take their wives back home.
One will sell his into prostitution.
The other's, deserted, will wander into it.

The men have business-like reserve.
They've always had it.
A few times in their careers
they've surfaced in places unlike theirs,
but nearer home, suspicion lingers after them :
the odd, faintly-puzzled question aired
when their trace, like some odd, faint smell,
has disappeared.
See her, their spiritual mother, duck
out of the car and stalk forward,

cameras and mikes straining towards her.
Once she rose
– she was always rising – to the occasion;
now she is to say nothing.
She, too, is a presence.

The last time the men are together
– crisps trodden into the carpet,
beer cans and boxes crumpled under the sofa -
they see her on the screen
and, with a faint sneer of recogntion,
that they did all right by her.

But it is the last time.

A few months later, one will die in a crash.
Seven years on, the other will be shot in his car.
In a society that has and does too much
and, knowing too little, goes too far,
like her,
they came, they did, they went.

One of the girls will return to Thailand,
a mother of two.
Of the other one, nothing is known.

## WINTER FACING STREET
*Betül Tarıman, Türkiye*
*Translated by Hasan Yayan, Türkiye*


the balcony overlooking the winter is my childhood.
the waters shivered as they cried.
what frothy joy?
what love drinker?
drunk snuggles inside.
a little joy, a little sad.
every time I reach for a dream.
aged with grief.

soil smells dry time
silence of the moment overflowed
to colorless vase
hiding the body with water
sibling with pain

mountain facing street
neither my mother nor myself
chosen courtyard
singing bazaar
engaged with loneliness

## KIŞA BAKAN SOKAK
*Betül Tarıman, Türkiye*


kışa bakan balkon çocukluğumdur
ağlarken sular ürpermiş
ne köpürtmüş sevinci
ne aşk tiryakisi
içinde sarhoş kuytular
biraz mahur biraz hüzzam
ne zaman rüyaya uzasam
kederle eskitilmiştir

kurak zaman kokmuştur toprak
taşmıştır anın sessizliği
renksiz bir vazoya
gövdesini suyla gizlemiş
acıyla kardeştir

dağa bakan sokak
ne annemdir ne kendim
avludur seçilir
çarşıdır söylenir
hayat içine eksilmiş
yalnızlıkla sözlenmiştir

# WINTER LOVE

*Burkhard P. Bierschenck, Germany*


What drives the hot desires
in the cold winter snow,
what is heating the love
on the reflecting ice?
Crushing the cold mirror
hurts young and aged.

Oh my beautiful winter love,
My precious snow crystal,
floating down into the valley,
Your feeling so fragile,
where spring turns green,
 and morning wind passes.

## WINTERLIEBE
*Burkhard P. Bierschenck, Deutschland*

Was treibt die heißen Wünsche
im kalten Winterschnee,
was heizt die Liebe an
auf dem blinkenden Eis?
Den kalten Spiegel zertrümmern,
das schmerzt jung und alt.

Oh meine schöne Winterliebe,
Mein kostbarer Schneekristall,
hinunter ins Tal schwebend,
Deine Gefühle so zerbrechlich,
wo der Frühling grün wird,
der Morgenwind weht vorbei.

THE CIRCLE
*Chloe Koutsoubelli, Greece*


In the middle of a deadly summer
with large mosquitoes
helicopters over our heads,
two billion tons of ice melting
in the blink of an eye,
while the dinosaurs
still fret over a blind comet
and people around a fire
whisper songs,
winter is not a season for us,
it's an era,
it's a story long forgotten
it' s a circle.
Whatever has been, will come again.
And you will learn once again
to draw my name on the walls
of the cave.
And maybe this time
after all these centuries
the endangered species of your smile
will survive the ice age.
And maybe just for once,
winter will not come for us.

Ο ΚΥΚΛΟΣ
*Χλόη Κουτσουμπέλη, Ελλάδα*


Στο μέσον ενός θανάσιμου καλοκαιριού
με μεγάλα κουνούπια- ελικόπτερα
πάνω απ΄ τα κεφάλια μας,
καθώς δισεκατομμύρια τόνοι πάγου
λιώνουν σ΄ένα μόνο βλεφάρισμα,
οι δεινόσαυροι ανησυχούν για έναν τυφλό κομήτη
και οι άνθρωποι γύρω απ' την φωτιά
ψιθυρίζουν τραγούδια,
ο χειμώνας δεν είναι μία ακόμα εποχή,
είναι ολόκληρη χρονική περίοδος,
ιστορία ξεχασμένη από καιρό,
κύκλος.
Ό, τι υπήρξε, θα υπάρξει ξανά.
Κι εσύ απ΄ την αρχή θα μάθεις
τ' όνομά μου να ζωγραφίζεις
στους τοίχους της σπηλιάς.
Και ίσως αυτή την φορά
μετά από τόσους αιώνες,
το χαμόγελό σου -είδος υπό εξαφάνιση-
καταφέρει να επιβιώσει
στην εποχή των παγετώνων,
και ίσως για μια μόνο φορά
ο χειμώνας να μην έρθει για μας.

WINTERLOVE
*Christine Geweke, Germany*
*Translated by Detlef Abraham, Germany*


you will be my last love. my heart and my
mind not strong enough for repeats, palpitations
doubts and dying kisses. so I paint us
into the sea of moments. you are my stoker
of the old steamship my dearest captain


at night in your arms I will be your greyly girl.
my braids a rope which combines our memories
to one whole and our love a star down which
unified the heaven with the sea at
the horizon together with your love

WINTERLIEBE
*Christine Geweke, Deutschland*


du wirst meine letzte liebe sein. mein herz und mein
    verstand
nicht mehr stark genug für wiederholungen,
    herzrasen, zweifel
und sterbende küsse. so male ich uns ins meer der
    augenblicke
du bist mein heizer im alten dampfschiff, mein
    liebster kapitän


nachts in deinen armen werde ich dein graues
    mädchen sein,
meine zöpfe ein tauwerk, dass unsere erinnerungen zu
    einer
einheit verbindet und unsere liebe ein
    sternenuntergang der
 mit dir am horizont den himmel mit dem meer vereint

UP HOUR X
*Claudia Piccinno, Italy*


If I could sit in the hollow of your arms
like a mollusk in a concave shell
without thoughts or anxieties to obey.
If I could believe in fairy tales,
in Trilly's magic dust.
If only I could count happy commitments,
instead of filling out health bulletins.
If ... If ... If ...
Infinite is the ramble of the mind
when prospects are others.
I have counted the reserves for the winter
that you had accumulated in the garage
and I wonder if they will be enough
until the hour x.
What a heavy load you left us,
the preparations for another farewell.

# FINO ALL'ORA X
*Claudia Piccinno, Italia*

Se io potessi accomodarmi
nell'incavo delle tue braccia
come mollusco in una concava conchiglia
senza pensieri ne ansie a cui obbedire.
Se io potessi credere alle favole,
alla polvere magica di Trilly.
Se solo potessi contare gli impegni felici,
anzichè compilare bollettini sanitari.
Se… Se… Se…
Infinito è il vaneggiare della mente
quando le prospettive sono altre.
Ho contato le riserve per l'inverno
che avevi accumulato in garage
e mi domando
se basteranno fino all'ora x.
Che carico pesante ci hai lasciato,
i preparativi per un altro addio.

FUGITIVE
*Cordula Scheel, Germany*
*Translated by Barry Stevenson, United Kingdom*


Who knows the way still open
Among  so many ?
You  fled  the murdering hordes
Got lost in  yourself
 Not at home anymore
In your own skin

You listen  in
With open mouth
To the moon's  weak light
The heavens no longer
Dawn and fade
No-one  calls your name

FLÜCHTIG
*Cordula Scheel, Deutschland*


Wer weiß den noch offenen Weg
unter vielen?
Du flohst vor den mordenden Horden
gehst fremd mit dir selbst
daheim nicht mehr
in der eigenen Haut

Du lauschst
mit offenem Mund
in das Unlicht des Mondes
hier geht kein Himmel mehr
ein und aus
niemand ruft dich mit Namen

DESIRE
*Dalia Staponkutė, Lithuania*
*Translated from German version*
*by Barry Stevenson, United Kingdom*


The grammar of the new age
With its prevailing subjunctive
Bears witness to our transience
Like the timeless
We can be killed no longer
As in the tales
Of stolen love
But we could maybe
Kill each other
If we wanted to
Subtly, in a titillating way
From a distance

Our age-old desire strides
Through the medieval town
As it always will
It will come again
For ejected from
The path of time
It is without measure
It is fathomless
No longer ours
And its recurrence cannot
Be erased

GEISMAS
*Dalia Staponkutė, Lietuva*


Naujojo laiko gramatika,
kur vyrauja tariamoji nuosaka,
liudys, kad tapome belaikiai
ir mūsų, belaikių,
niekas nebegalės nužudyti
kaip tose pasakose
apie pavogtą meilę.
Tačiau galėsime
jeigu panorėsime
žudyti vienas kitą
pikantiškai ir subtiliai,
iš tolo.

Mūsų buvusi aistra žingsniuoja
per viduramžių miestą.
Peržengia mus.
Ir taip jau visad bus –
ji kartosis
nuo pradžių
nes, išmušta iš laiko vėžių,
ji nebeišmatuojama, bedugnė
mums nebepriklauso
ir jokie pasikartojimai
jos neištrins.

DECEMBER
*Domenico Pisana, Italy*
*Translated by Floriana Ferro, Italy*


Before the glass I look at this December sky
in its gait of growing clouds, looking for the sense
of the whisper of small birds gathering on the hill,
in the dense twilight of my heart I murmur the breath
of the air, the leaves are scattered
under the light gaze of the sun.

And now I'm troubled by the progress of the worst
    indifference,
the space of walls gets more and more high, the glory
lights the fire to burn interactions, the star
drunk with applauses raises his scepter of truth
and the poet crumbles in his chest the images
he dreamt about to the edge.

I feel a missing person in the wood of suspects,
the fog doesn't loosen its slithering haze on the valley,
the night looks out over visions and revisions of the
    new day
and I board on patience ships sailing through the seas
of misunderstanding waiting for Someone
who gives me the courtesy of language.

I need resistance against the attacks of Barbarians, hawks lying
in the media circus, peacocks behind the keyboards
doling out judgements; I feel myself like a plough
cutting through the soil, somebody should spread the seed, splash it
with the water of truth, look after the stems,
others will collect fruits of good in the future world.

And the rain will come in winter to flood ditches of falsehood,
to touch the mohawks of pitiless men,
to soften the soil which is thirsty for the summer heat,
to grow the novel we're bringing inside ourselves
passing through the cold season waiting for spring
and for the smell of hay among the murmur of swallows.

# DICEMBRE
*Domenico Pisana,Italia*


In questo cielo di dicembre che osservo dai vetri
nel suo incedere di nuvole crescenti, cerco il senso
del sussurro di piccoli volatili che s'affollano sul
   colle,
nella densa penombra del mio cuore sospiro il
   bisbiglio
dell'aria, le foglie si disperdono
sotto lo sguardo lieve del sole.

E ora m'inquieta l'avanzare del male
   dell'indifferenza,
lo spazio di muri che si fanno sempre più alti, la gloria
che accende il fuoco per bruciare relazioni, la stella
ubriaca di applausi che alza lo scettro della verità
e il poeta frantuma nel petto le sue immagini
sognate nel limite.

E allora mi sento un disperso nel bosco dei sospetti,
la nebbia non allenta la foschia che scivola sulla
   vallata,
s'affaccia la notte tra visioni e revisioni del nuovo
   giorno
e m' imbarco su navi di pazienza nei mari
dell'incomprensione in attesa che Qualcuno
   mi doni il garbo della lingua.

Ci vuole resistenza all'assalto dei barbari, falchi
    sdraiati
nei salotti mediatici, pavoni dietro le tastiere
che dispensano sentenze; io mi sento soltanto un
    aratro
che solca la terra, ci vuole chi sparga il seme, chi lo
    annaffi
con l'acqua della verità, chi custodisca gli steli,
altri raccoglieranno frutti di bene nel tempo che verrà.
E verrà la pioggia d'inverno ad allagare i fossati di
    menzogne,
a lambire le creste d'uomini privi di pietà,
ad ammorbidire la terra ancora assetata dall'afa estiva,
a far sbocciare il romanzo che ci portiamo dentro
attraversando la stagione del freddo in attesa della
    primavera
e dell'odore del fieno tra il murmure di rondini.

# THIRST FOR PEACE

*Dorel Cosma, Romania*
*Translated by Zorin Diaconescu, Romania*

I look in the mirror
sequentially.
I wait for the blast
to shine
every thought,
every moment.
I'm trying to worry about the
cruel taste.
No smoke,
no cold,
no harm.
I burn.
I am accompanied
by pain,
by joy.
I am at your disposal:
Thirst for peace!
Alongside me,
a lantern
keeps the balance.
It watches!

## SETE DE LINIȘTE
*Dorel Cosma, România*

Privesc în oglindă
secvențial.
Aștept erupția
să lumineze
fiecare gând,
fiecare clipă.
Mă încearcă neliniștea
gustului crud.
Fără fum,
fără să frigă,
fără să rănească.
Ard.
Mă însoțesc
durerile,
bucuriile.
Sunt la dispoziția ta:
Sete de liniște !
Lângă mine,
un felinar
menține echilibrul.
Veghează!

# BLURRED SIGHT
*Elizabeth Kurian 'Mona', India*


I see through my spectacles
And read through those lenses
Sometimes I wonder if the dimness today
Is because of my deteriorating sight
Or whether my glasses are covered with dust

People see the world through media-glasses
The TV, internet, social media, newspapers,
They wonder if what they are made to consume
Is really the truth, whether good or bad news
Or if dust has been sprayed on the media -glasses
So that people read, hear and believe
What those in power wish them to .

Whenever a person's sight seems to be deficient
Spectacles can be cleaned or the lenses replaced
But what options do people have to know the truth
When they fear they are not being shown the reality?

# CHANGE IN STATUS
*Elizabeth Kurian 'Mona', Indian.*


You are a beautiful damsel with a mind of your own
I said you could choose when to tie the nuptial knot
But I am your guardian, I have waited too long
You have not changed as was my wish and hope
Now I shall treat you like a wayward child
Browbeat you, lock you up and force you to marry
A strong man that I have chosen for you
It is for your own good, you will see.

If your heart breaks, it is none of my concern
If you feel like a prisoner, it is not my problem
If I have not taken your consent, you know why
You will be happy bye and bye with your new status

You think it was arbitrary and illegal, my dear,
I make laws and twist them to suit myself
You belong to me, it is your duty to obey
My actions may be wrong but power is mine
It for your good, you must try to understand
If you do not, more trouble will be in store
Should I dwell on this topic anymore?

COMET

*Emel Koşar, Turkey*
*Translated by Yasemin Üşümüş, Turkey*


you are looking with all the shades of blue
as i lose my grasp on you any time
as if you lock the cumulative memories
to a timid raindrop
as if you solve the disappointed messages of planet
  without saving
as if you turn the exhausted nights of winter to spring
the echo of snow flakes is in my warm skin
lets write a history with our lyric voice

# KUYRUKLU YILDIZ
*Emel Koşar, Türkiye*


mavinin bütün tonlarıyla bakıyorsun
her an avuçlarımdan kayıp gidecekmiş gibi
biriken anıları ürkek bir yağmur damlasına
  hapsedercesine
kırgın gezegen mesajlarını kaydetmeden çözercesine
yorgun kış gecelerini bahara döndürürcesine
kar tanelerinin yankısı ılık tenimde
hadi tarih yazalım lirik sesimizle

# DECEMBER IN BOSNIA

*Emina Čabaravdić-Kamber, Bosnia and Herzegovina*
*Translated by Gino Leineweber, Germany*


A feeble fire trembles in the chimney
A sign
The embers are slowly
Turning to ashes

The deep night softly
Sneaks into the room

The weak embers
Draw in a gloomy chamber
A picture on the ceiling
Like a stage decoration

Outside snowflakes swinging in the wind
Lights of the lanterns intoxicating themselves
Twirling around
On snow-covered stone

It is December

In front of the cloudy window panes
Swaying in the white veil
The bare branches of poplars

Frost has painted
A heart on the window pane
As in a fairy tale

It is December

# DEZEMBER IN BOSNIEN
*Emina Čabaravdić-Kamber, Bosnien-Herzegowina*


Im Kamin zittert ein schwaches Feuer
Ein Zeichen
Dass die Glut langsam
Zur Asche wird

Tiefe Nacht schleicht sich
Sacht in den Raum

Die schwache Glut
Zeichnet im halbdunklen Zimmer
Ein Bild an die decke
Wie die Kulisse einer Bühne

Draußen wiegen sich Schneeflocken im Wind
Lichter der Laternen berauschen
Sich im Tanz
Auf schneebedecktem Stein

Es ist Dezember

Vor den trüben Fensterscheiben
Wiegen sich im weißen Schleier
Die kahlen Äste der Pappeln

Der Frost hat ein Herz
Auf die Fensterscheibe gemalt
Wie in einem Märchen

Es ist Dezember

THE SNOWDROP
*Ester Cecere, Italy*
*Translated by Claudia Piccinno, Italia*

The winter didn't win you
on the steep slope
even more ruthless.
Nor the blanket of snow
hardened by the mistral
has stopped you.
You melted the crystal
of your icy blanket,
fragile yet strong
you were outcropping.

# IL BUCANEVE
*Ester Cecere, Italia*


Non ti ha vinto l'inverno
sul ripido pendio
ancor più spietato.
Né ti ha fermato
della neve la coltre
dal maestrale indurita.
Della tua gelida coperta
i cristalli hai fuso,
fragile
eppur fortissimo
affiorando.

# ON THE FLOWER RIGHT OVER THERE
*Fethi Sassi, Tunisia*


I won't be sleeping early tonight;
I'll stay in bed and imagine lovely things instead.
I'll pretend that I'm sitting cross-legged on the edge of
   a poem to wait for the evening train.
I'll also pretend that I'm sitting in a park
Looking at a tree on its knees.
The words drip from its branch,
That branch that carried many butterflies.
They meet every spring...
But far away,
On the flower right over there,
A butterfly is lying down alone;
It's the one that forgot its wings on the edge of a
   poem
As the evening train was passing by .

عَلى زَهرَةٍ هُناكَ
الشَّاعر : فتحي ساسي
الجنسية : تونسية


لنْ أنَامَ بَاكرا هَذِه اللّيلة..
سَأبقَى في فِراشِي لأتَخيّلَ أشيَاءَ جمَيلةً .
سَأتَوهَّمُ أنّي أتَربَّعُ عَلَى حَافةِ قَصِيدَةٍ ، لأنتَظرَ قِطَارَ المسَاءِ.
وَأتَوهَّمُ كَذلكَ أنّني أجلِسُ في حَدِيقَةٍ كَبيرَةٍ،
أنظُرُ إلى شَجرَةٍ تجلسُ عَلَى ركبتَيهَا،
فَتتَقَاطَرُ مِنْ غُصنهَا الكَلماتُ .
الغُصنُ الّذي حَملَ فَراشَاتٍ كَثيرةً
تَلتَقي كُلَّ رَبيعٍ....
لكنْ بَعيدًا هُناكَ...
عَلَى زَهرَةٍ هُناكَ ....
فَراشَةٌ تَقبعُ وَحِيدَةً.
تِلكَ الّتي نَسيَتْ جَنَاحَيهَا عَلَى حَافَّةِ قَصِيدَةٍ،
حِينَ مَرَّ قِطارُ المسَاءِ.

# THE COTTAGE
*Gino Leineweber, Germany*


He found his way into the mountains
Snow caps and all and a cottage below the peaks
It didn't seem so far away
But vanished and reappeared
It happened again and again
He was wandering all the ups and downs
And wondering whether he might be
On a path which wasn't as safe as he thought


Then maybe—may be at the sunset
While the giver of life was inflaming the sky and
    clouds
He thought he was doomed
For painting the canvas of the mountains
Only to erase it with darkness that had fallen
From the height of the universe
Wiping out every colorful image
Bringing on him cold and death—maybe


In the morning it shines again
As though there hasn't been a night or darkness
Or even a yesterday either
He or another self that pretends to be him
Is on the way again into the mountains

Is meeting green, green grass and flowers in yellow
    and blue
Is listening to the whisper of distant falls and busy
    bees
Happy since there hasn't been a word about the
    cottage—yet

## DIE HÜTTE
*Gino Leineweber, Deutschland*


Er war unterwegs in den Bergen
Schneefelder und eine Hütte vor dem Gipfel
Sieht nicht so weit aus
Doch sie verschwindet und erscheint
Wieder und wieder
Er wanderte durch Höhen und Tiefen
Vielleicht war er gar nicht auf einem Weg
Der so sicher war wie er gedacht hatte


Denn vielleicht – wenn die Sonne untergeht
Wenn sich Himmel und Wolken bemalen
Wäre er dem Untergang geweiht
Wenn auf der Leinwand der  Berge
Die Farben sich später
In die Finsternis hüllen
Und von der Höhe des Universums
Ihm Kälte und Tod bereiten – vielleicht


Im Morgen leuchtet es wieder
Als hätte es nie eine Finsternis gegeben
Oder gar ein Gestern
Er oder ein anderes Selbst das vorgibt er zu sein
Ist wieder unterwegs in den Bergen

Nun trifft er auf grünes Grass und Blumen in Gelb
und Blau
Horcht auf das Wispern von Bienen und fernen
Wasserfällen
Er ist glücklich – und kein Wort von einer Hütte

WINTER SPEECH
*Hilal Karahan, Turkey*


He saw the anxiety, which was a mountain village
under her eyelashes. An ivy has covered the mouth
of the well with its root and seeds. Yet her tongue
and teeth are a snapdragon during kissing.

He wanted to touch her cheek
with the magic of a wet sign;
the heat of his palm turned to ice:

"Why do probabilities sting us, does anger sharpen
expectation? Is love a test for our spirits?"

He stared at her and then turned outside:

"How many worlds can be in an earth?
Wherever I went, I always take myself with me.
Be disturbed by my presence."


The tired wind has fallen down
along decayed leaves. A death corpse
was being dragged by the ants.
The sky was going continuously.
A storm would start.

The grass didn't notice anything.

KIŞ KONUŞMASI
*Hilal Karahan, Türkiye*


Kaygıyı gördü kirpiklerinin altında dağ köyü.
Örtmüştü kuyunun üstünü
köklenen, tohuma durmuş sarmaşık.
Oysa dili, o dişleri öpüşürken aslanağzı…

Islak bir izin büyüsüyle yanağına uzandı,
buz kesti avcunun sıcaklığı:

"İhtimaller niye acıtır ki?
Öfke, beklentiyi mi biler insanda?
Ruhların sınanması mı aşk?"

Kıyasıya baktı adam, bir kadına, bir dışarıya:

"Kaç yer yüzünden oluşabilir ki arzküre?
Nereye gitsem, kendimi de yanımda götürdüm.
Rahatsız ol varlığımdan."

Aşağılara düştü yorulan rüzgâr, çürümüş
yaprakların arasına. Ölü bir gövdeyi
sürüklüyordu karıncalar. Gökyüzü hiç
durmadan gidiyordu. Koptu kopacaktı fırtına.


Haberi olmadı otların.

# LOOK BOTH WAYS BEFORE CROSSING
*Holly Iglesias, USA*

Winter was upon us, heavy as the sweater he wore to anatomy lectures, the blue one that smelled like *tabaco negro* and *Varon Dandy* even after I washed it in the sink. Alone each day in a Spartan apartment—table, two chairs, bed, radio, books in English that arrived two months after I did—*Joy of Cooking*, Rimbaud's *Illuminations*, The *Annotated Alice*—I busied myself making lists of Spanish nouns and irregular verbs until he arrived home with the other men and the building came alive with conversation and the sounds of forks beating eggs and furniture shifted for dinner after which everyone climbed into bed before the furnace went off for the night; until the day, putting away the laundry, I felt a stack of slim books behind his socks, diaries—1969 green, 1970 blue, 1971 red, and one yet to be written, 1972 beige— beige, which seemed all wrong for the now of us, for the newness of us, for the wide wide ocean between us and home, the word still catching in my throat though it had been drained of meaning for him years before, which is why he began his search for a wife, a tale of woe described in detail in the final pages of 1971—the plan, the names, the proposals and rejections—until he asked me on the first day of the following, the beige and the still blank, year.

# WINTER AND SADNESS
*Jenny Lkhagvasuren, Mongolia*


The signs of winter ahead
Make me feel blue
Bringing one more year to my age
Makes me hasty, but I still have not done anything
No good reputation,
No honor,
And no service for others yet another winter
I feel upset
I think last year
I was saddened by the hearsay of the winter
As time goes by
I rush into anything
Then I will become
As white as snow of the winter

# ӨВӨЛ, ГУНИГ ХОЁР
*Jenny Lkhagvasuren, Mongγol Ulus*

Айсуй өвлийн чимээнээр
Гуниг сэдрэнэ
Ахиад нэг нас нэмнэ гэхээр
Адгаж яарна
Алдар ч үгүй
Гавъяа ч үгүй
Ач тус ч үгүй
Ахин нэг өвөлтэй золгоно гэхээр
Сэтгэлээр унана
Өмнөх өвлийн сургаар ч
Бас л ингэж
Гуниглаж, бачимдаж байсан биз
Цаг хугацаа эргэдгээрээ эргээд л
Тэр тоолонд яаран адгаад л
Тэгээд нэг л мэдэхэд
Цал буурал өвөл шигээ болно

# WINTRY

*Juan C. Tajes, Uruguay/Netherland*

> Now is the winter of our discountent
> Made glorious summer…
> William Shakespeare/Richard III


Now the winter of our discontent is not literary
and the bodies vomited by the black waters
are not a metaphor for violence
that rages with the fugitives of violence.
Words sound hollow and insufficient,
gestures, fuss without meaning.
Nobody illuminates the night, nobody opens his soul,
   nobody,
but the dead are alone at the shores of the world,
They no longer dream, they no longer wait.
The wet motionless shadow
over mud and sand and trash,
under a pale and blind moon,
stopped at the minute of the last breath,
that will be erased with the first light
in the gray morning of not fulfilled fate.
The winter will be even longer
our discontent will be more profound
and the summer less glorious.

INVERNAL
*Juan C. Tajes, Uruguay/Holanda*


> Ahora el invierno de nuestro descontento
> Hace más glorioso el verano...
> William Shakespeare/Ricardo III


Ahora el invierno de nuestro descontento no es
    literario
y los cuerpos vomitados por las negras aguas
no son metáfora de la violencia encarnizada
que se ensaña con los fugitivos de la violencia.
Las palabras suenan huecas e insuficientes,
los gestos,  aspavientos sin sentido.
Nadie ilumina la noche, nadie abre su alma, nadie,
pero los muertos están solos en las orillas del mundo,
Ya no sueñan, ya no esperan.
La húmeda sombra inmóvil
sobre el barro y la arena y la morralla,
bajo luna pálida y ciega,
es sombra detenida en el instante del último aliento,
que será borrada con la primera luz
en la mañana gris del destino no cumplido.
El invierno será aún más largo,
será más hondo nuestro descontento
y menos glorioso el verano.

THE NAKED CITY
*Julio Pavanetti, Uruguay/Spain*
*Translated by Annabel Villar and Gabriela Pavanetti,*
*Spain*


A nostalgic breeze from the river
climbs up the oldest streets,
diluting in the square the wild sea
and the suspicion of the moon is clear reflection,
guessed on its back
unblemished of any prejudice.

The deserted city draws by hand
filaments of transparent rain
that descend into the pit of the night.

City with a sovereign past,
slightly inclined to sadness,
lashed by the gusts of the wind
that crosses the Square
and lets itself down,
–blind and like a dead body–
to the gloom, like fine drizzle falls
rolling deafly through the streets
which smell like a night in a city,
naked now as the eternal Comala.[1]


1 Comala is the imaginary city that the Mexican writer Juan Rulfo
mentions in his novel "Pedro Páramo"

Silence at the innocent balconies
with wavy iron railings
anointed by the air of the years.

Silence in the corners which hurry up
nostalgic attacks of night jasmine time.

The naked city gets wet slowly,
filling its profile with the humidity
that covers up the echoes of a past
of haughty looks
and birds of geometric and bold flights.

The naked city, when the night
imposes its power, drops its eyelids
and undertakes a new journey into memory.

## LA CIUDAD DESNUDA
Julio Pavanetti, Uruguay/España


Una brisa de río y de nostalgia
asciende por las calles más antiguas,
diluyendo en la plaza el mar bravío
y la sospecha de un reflejo claro
de luna, que se adivina a su espalda,
inmaculada de todo prejuicio.

Desierta la ciudad dibuja a mano
filamentos de lluvia transparente
que descienden al pozo de la noche.

Ciudad con un pasado soberano,
levemente inclinada a la tristeza,
azotada por ráfagas de un viento
que atraviesa la Plaza y se descuelga
ciego, y a cuerpo muerto, a la penumbra,
igual que cae la fina llovizna
rodando sordamente por las calles
que huelen a noche en una ciudad
hoy desnuda como Comala[2] eterna.
Silencio en los balcones inocentes
con sus barandas de hierro ondulado
ungidas por el aire de los años.


2 Comala es la ciudad imaginaria que el escritor mexicano Juan
Rulfo menciona en su novela "Pedro Páramo"

Silencio en las esquinas que apresuran
los embates nostálgicos de un tiempo
de nocturnos jazmines del país.

Desnuda la ciudad se moja lenta,
poblando su perfil de una humedad
que enmascara los ecos de un pasado
de miradas altivas, y de pájaros
de vuelos geométricos y audaces.

Desnuda la ciudad, cuando la noche
impone su poder, baja sus párpados
y emprende un nuevo viaje hacia el recuerdo.

## THIS TOO SHALL PASS
*K Pankajam, India*


We cross over to a land that does not talk our tongue.
Theirs  we learn to express in banal ways possible.
Straddling in two worlds, we are neither here nor
   there
Yet try to mingle with the new culture, hoping for the
   best.

The sea we cross is not docile or kind
In its depths we toss our longing for our own homes.
It devours our dreams, oftentimes our toddlers too
The whales of the sea can hear our cries.

Our women are scared of men who forgot mercy,
Forgot their mothers, forgot sisters, forgot humanity.
They drink their own tears and eat their own flesh
Pain of homesickness or melancholy of racism,  rather
   easy to abate.
Mothers who saw the ugly rage of throwing their
   children out of the windows
Could only pray for their kids' lives,  knew only if
   luck favours.

Wind says,  keep moving; cloud says, don't brood
Rain says don't allow your dreams to die
Sky says, the world is one;  the sun says, keep your
   hopes high

And the sea says, the shore is somewhere near.

Let's not close the doors of our hearts;  let them write
    their own poems
Picking up the threads of their shattered dreams from
    the shards.

NEXT
*Liana Sakelliou, Greece*


I Aphrodite

Eva has dark eyes and hair
a black tattooed dragon on her heart.
She speaks with the essential grace

that enters her goddess,  has the taste
of the giant's blood on her lips.
She loves that she cannot love.

Running the lance through his body
Eva forces her way into the past—
herself in the present so much.


II Artemis

Cold morning at the museum mountain
the goddess –strong and absolute—
commands the animals to hunt.

Tillman's dusky eyes watch her
draped body enter the cave
her marble flexible and muscled

touches him
and the intrusion of words
exists in a new way.


III Apollon

He brings radiance to the museum
a young man called Apollo
now in Berlin he speaks

including the specifics of music and light.
The camera on eye, ear, temple
fragments his lance, records him upside down.

Now he breathes like the beating of Icarian wings.
No lyre, pomegranate, wreath or bird.
No blood.


IV Poet

Athens, Pergamon—
Gigantomachy in London, in Berlin—
a marble libation to power
but what can you tell me
of that season of promise?
Computer's warm breath
has faith in miracles—

in deep winter is forming an identity
suspended like an extended lance.


Notes
Επόησεν: Made it - an inscription on the frieze of the Pergamon
Monument.
Eva Meckback, Tilman Strauss: German actors filmed while
reading the Pergamon Poems by the German poet Gerhard
Falkner.

ΕΠΟΗΣΕΝ
*Λιάνα Σακελλίου, Ελλάδα*


I   Αφροδίτη


Η Εύα έχει σκούρα μαλλιά και μάτια
μαύρο δράκο τατουάζ στην καρδιά.
Μιλά με την χάρη

που διακρίνει τη θεά της
κι έχει τη γεύση του αίματος στα χείλη—
αγαπά που δεν μπορεί ν' αγαπήσει.

Σπρώχνοντας το ακόντιο μέσα στο σώμα του
η Εύα μπαίνει με βία στο παρελθόν—
στο παρόν τόσο πολύ όμως.


II   Άρτεμις


Κρύο πρωί στο μουσείο.
Στην κορυφή του βουνού του
η αχλή ξεδιπλώνεται στη

βιαιότητα του λευκού
και η θεά –δυνατή και απόλυτη—
διατάζει τα ζώα να κυνηγήσουν.
Τα σκοτεινά μάτια του Τίλμαν

ακολουθούν το πτυχωμένο της σώμα
στη σπηλιά

το μάρμαρό της εύκαμπτα τον αγγίζει
και η επιβολή των λέξεων
αρχίζει να υπάρχει διαφορετικά.


III   Απόλλων

Ακτινοβολεί το μουσείο
ένας νέος ονόματι Απόλλων
τώρα στο Βερολίνο συνομιλεί

με όλες τις λεπτομέρειες της μουσικής και του φωτός.
Η κάμερα κεντράρει στον κρόταφο, στο αυτί,  στο
   μάτι
τεμαχίζει το ακόντιο, τον αντιστρέφει.

Τώρα αναπνέει σαν το Ικάριο φτερό.
Χωρίς λύρα, ρόδι ή στεφάνι.
Χωρίς αίμα.


IV Ποιητής

Αθήναι, Πέργαμος—
η Γιγαντομαχία στο Λονδίνο, στο Βερολίνο—
μαρμάρινη σπονδή στην εξουσία

όμως εσύ τι θα πεις
για την εποχή εκείνη της υπόσχεσης;
Η ζεστή ανάσα του υπολογιστή

πιστεύει σε θαύματα—
στον βαθύ χειμώνα σχηματίζει μια ταυτότητα—
αιωρείται σαν προτεταμένη λόγχη.

REAPPRAISAL
*Lily Exarchopoulou, Greece*
*To Vassilis Gouroyannis*


Now that the books end up serving  as firewood
And the words spread out  fester meanings
But still the sun insists on  rising from the East
Now that winter is settling in
and you ask for human comfort
I'm outraged, contracted into BEING


Broken by unuttered feelings
Engulfed by insurgent powers
Induced into spleen melancholy
Nullified by the inhumanity that persists
Grumbling constantly with one's self


Fffff blowing into the fire
Fffff expecting a miracle


Since you are an unbeliever
You'll  proceed alone in the deep winter
Slosh about in the broken water pipes
VICTORIOUS

ΑΝΑΨΗΛΑΦΗΣΗ
*Λίλυ Εξαρχοπούλου, Ελλάδα*
*Στον Βασίλη Γκουρογιάννη*

Τώρα που τα βιβλία καταλήγουνε καυσόξυλα
Κι οι λέξεις σκορπίζουν κακοφορμισμένο νόημα
Όμως ο ήλιος από ανατολάς εμμένει να ανατέλλει
Τώρα που χειμώνιασε κι η θαλπωρή σ' ανθρώπους
Έξαλλη συναιρούμαι στο ΥΠΑΡΧΩ

Ύψιλον κεφαλαίο της Υποταγής
Πι παρασιτικό της Προσαρμογής
Άλφα του Άγχους των προηγουμένων
Ρο με το κροτάλισμα του τρόμου
Χι που καταλήγει στο Χαραμίζομαι
Ωμέγα διό Εσύ το Άλφα και το Ωμέγα

Φου φου τα βιβλία στη φουφού
Φου φου και θα γίνει το θαύμα

Αφού δεν πιστεύεις
Μόνος θα πορευτείς στη βαρυχειμωνιά
Θα πλατσουρίσεις
στους σπασμένους σωλήνες
ΝΙΚΗΤΗΣ

A HAPPY LONER
*Magie Faure-Vidot Vijay-Kumar, Seychelloise*


We are all free birds
In so outreached worlds
Where all become one
Same our parents when young

Some prefer "charlatanism"
Others, the "ISM"
Whilst egotism
Refuses to spell PRISM

Be audacious
Not frivolous
Off-road
Is no best mode

# A CALL FOR RESPECT AND PEACE
*Magie Faure-Vidot Vijay-Kumar, Seychelloise*


Let us be proud
Of a clean and well-done job
We all perform
To earn a decent living
Remember that all jobs are noble
Except those involving crimes, lies, betrayals,
  bribery, cheatings and some others
Let us respect all human beings, nature, animals,
plants and respect for a peaceful living

## BURIED TOO LONG
*Maja Herman Sekulić, Serbia/USA*


January is the cruellest month, after all,
It promises a new start
And begets not a bud.
The curtain fell. Or,
There was none . Only
Lights down. The end of
The Waste Land? I exit
The run-down Liberty,
Thinking of the absurdity of
Stage productions of the Modernist poetry.

I descend to underground
In front of the new Disney store on
Forty Second Street. Stop –
Here is the Wasteland. No
Need for il miglior fabbro
To fragment it even more. No need.
Unreal City.
Down, in your underbelly, a Latino
Dances tango Argentino with
A woman-size doll, cariño
Stuck to his shoes, helpless,
Flipping her dead body, graceless,
Everyone's eyes on her panties
And her clumsy legs made of rags
As if they are part of a peep show

From the street above.

This Sunday winter did keep us warm,
Covering the city in fog, cutting
Skyscrapers to a human size, with no sky to touch.
We had dim sum in Chinatown.
His eyes were like jade. Transparent
Shimmering, with my light upon them, wide open.
– I will show you the road – he said.

Monday brought the cold
And, the sun at last. Buried
Too long in the papers. I took
A walk and E-mailed
My dog,
Thanks to its good feng shui
My only plant
Fed itself.

## PREDUGO SAHRANJENA
*Maja Herman Sekulić, Srbija*


Januar je ipak najsuroviji mesec –
Obećava novo
Ne rađa ni pupoljak.
Zavesa je pala. Ili nije
Ni postojala. Samo su se
Svetla pogasila. Kraj
Puste zemlje? Izlazim
Iz oronulog pozorišta Liberti,
Razmišljam o apsurdu
Pozorišnih postavki
Modernističkog pesništva.

Spuštam se u podzemlje
Ispred nove radnje, „Diznijeve,"
Na četrdeset drugoj ulici. Stani –
Ovde je pusta zemlja –
Ne treba joj il miglior fabbro
da je bolje fragmentuje. Ne.
Nestvarni grade.

Dole, u tvom donjem trbuhu, Latino
Igra tango argentino, cariño,
Sa lutkom mesto žene
Zakačenom za cipele
Mrtvo joj se telo cima bez gracije
Svi joj gledaju u gaćice I krute noge krpene

Kao da su nastavak pornografske predstave
Sa nadzemlja ove ulica.

Ove nedelje zima nas je grejala,
Uvijajući grad u maglu, presecajući
Oblakodere na pola, bez neba da paraju.
Jeli smo dim sum u Kineskoj četvrti.
Oči mu behu kao od žada. Prozirne
Pod mojom svetlošću, sjajne, širom otvorene.
– Pokazaću ti put, reče.

Ponedeljak je doneo hladnoću
I, napokon, sunce. Predugo
Sahranjena među hartijama, krenuh
U šetnju i poslah e-mail
Mom psu.
U čast dobrog feng-šua
Moja se jedina biljka
Sama hranila.

SNOW EXPLOSION
*Mallika Chari, India.*


Behind the snow blanket many tales.
Sprouts allowed not to shoot up,
Buds allowed not to bloom,
Cold wind grabbing tightly,
Long hours in the hold of night,
could it be the helplessness of Nature?

Like the blow of chill wind
Accusing arguments,
Like the attack of snow showers
Blaming threats,
Like the cover of fog
Veiled faults,
Like the frozen snow,
Hardened society,
What could be the search of man here?

Flowery words forgetting to bloom,
Rays of thoughts cut off in the sprout,
Burden in mind pressing hard,
Vacant look staring into the hold of night,
Thus,Did the sound of him too freeze?

பனிவடைப்பு
மல்லிகா, இந்தியா.


பனிப்போர்வையின் பின் பல கதைகள்.
துளிரவிடாத குருத்துக்கள்,
மலரவிடாத மொட்டுக்கள்,
இறுக்கிபிடிக்கும் குளிர்காற்று,
இரவின் பிடியில் வெகுநேரம்,
இயற்கையின் தவிப்போ இது?

குளிர்காற்றின் வீச்சுப்போலும்
குறைசொற்றும் வாதங்கள்,
பனிமழையின் தாக்கல்போலும்
பழிசுமத்தும் பேச்சுக்கள்,
மூடுபனியின் போர்வை போலும்
முக்காடிட்ட தவறுகள்,
உறைந்த பனிபோலும்
வறண்ட சமுதாயத்தில்,
மனிதனின் தடேல்தான் எது?


துளிரிலேவெடெட்டப்பட்ட எண்ணக்கதிர்கள்,
மலரமறந்த வார்த்தைப் பூக்கள்,
அழுத்தி அமுக்கும் இதயச்சுமைகள்,
இரவின் பிடியில் வெறுப்புப்பார்வை,
இப்படியே இவன் ஒலியும்
    உறைந்துவிட்டதோ?

Edge
*Maren Schönfeld, Germany*
*Translated by Barry Stevenson, United Kingdom*


You shoot
a glance at me
I don't
catch it – it flies past
bounces on the ground
shatters into fragments

I shoot
a glance at you
you don't
catch it – it flies past
bounces on the ground
shatters into fragments

For a while
we shoot
each other glances
landing at our feet

standing bound
fast in a sea of shards

Bande
*Maren Schönfeld, Deutschland*
Aus *Die Peripherie des Lichts*, 2014, Wiesenburg Verlag


Du wirfst
mir einen Blick zu
ich fange
ihn nicht er fliegt vorbei
prallt auf den Boden
zerspringt

Ich werfe
dir einen Blick zu
du fängst
ihn nicht er fliegt vorbei
prallt auf den Boden
zerspringt

Eine Weile
werfen wir
uns Blicke
vor die Füße

stehen vertäut
im Scherbenmeer

SO WHAT
*Marian Eikelhof, The Netherlands*

Whatever, wherever
with you
or alone
the hour
the day
I don't really care
I will fall asleep
close my eyes for what I see
the cries of the world
it's suffering
it's despair
I don't hear, I don't see
my God is a better God than yours
he doesn't care about you
he cares about me
so as a matter of fact
I can close all my eyes
even when yours stay open
in your starless night
you are a nobody
a loser in life's play
so whatever, wherever
I don't really care
I will sleep quietly
as my God exists.

SO WHAT
*Marian Eikelhof, Nederland*

Wat maakt het uit
alleen
of met jou
het uur
de dag
ik slaap gewoon in
sluit mijn ogen
voor wat ik zie
de schreeuw van de wereld
haar wanhoop
hoor ik niet
mijn God is een betere God
dan die van jou
hij geeft me wat ik nodig heb
om jou geeft hij niet
dus kan ik al mijn ogen sluiten
ook als die van jou  open blijven  in je sterrenloze
  nacht
ben je een nobody
terwijl ik alles heb en het om mij draait
dus wat maakt het uit
alleen
met hem of met haar, ik slaap rustig in,
want mijn God bestaat.

# BALADE DANS LA NEIGE
*Mawar Marzuki, Malaysia*


Balade dans la neige
Strolling in the snow
you hold a little beam of light
into my naked sight
lumière du soleil
living under the sunshine
grasses never forget to green so green
like me
who never know those flood of cold dust
white snow so white
from heaven crushing on my covered head

yes
Balade dans la neige
stockinged boots and heavy foot
stalking deep into my ankle
the beautiful sense of numbness
not a sweat to permeate the density
of lethargy

Balade dans la neige
in the warm country of my mind

# BALADE DANS LA NEIGE
*Mawar Marzuki, Malay*


Balade dans la neige
berjalan di dalam salju
kau unjurkan sesuluh cahaya
ke mataku yang telanjang

lumière du soleil
aku yang hidup dikucup matahari setahun
rumput hijauku yang banjir dengan kehijauan
tidak pernah lupa untuk menghijau
seperti aku
yang tidak pernah tahu
banjir debu putih yang menimpa kepalamu
salju putih yang memutih
gugur dari syurga menimpa
kepalaku yang berselubung

ya!
Balade dans la neige
sepatu berstoking mengheret sepasang kaki berat
buku lali tenggelam dalam lapisan salju
indah rupanya tidak merasa apa apa
tanpa setitik peluhpun meresap
mengeringkan keletihan yang tumpat
Balade dans la neige
berjalan di dalam salju
negara fikirku yang hangat

# WAITING AROUND THE CORNER
*Mesut Şenol, Turkey*


Dilemmas cannot wait for the arrival of the right
  season
Diverting attention would not make it less torturous
We are destined to go through our fate's direction
Our eyes blue or black, our skin dark or light, useless

We tend to forget about many things in life
We have to, or else our future might look desperate
Love and hatred hoover and linger permanently on us
No advice might console us when we are in a dire
  stalemate

There are no true heroes or some miserable creatures
  in this world
Dignity and meanness may not go always side by side
The true inner and humane quality lie at the depths of
  the heart
Nobody but the eyes of a merciful beings could sense
  it

As we all know that the calamity proves to be winter-
  like
With its snow-white appearance. Warnings! We tend
  to ignore

Happily, or prosperously lived, would it matter in a
   real sense
If you cannot bring up brighter seasons after winter in
   your essence.

# KÖŞE BAŞINDA BEKLERKEN
*Mesut Şenol, Türkiye*


Açmazlar bekleyemez doğru mevsimin gelişini
Dikkatin başka yöne çekilmesi azaltmaz işkenceyi
Yürümek zorundayız kaderimizin çizdiği yolda
Gözlerimiz mavi ya da siyah, tenimiz koyu ya da açık,
   ne fayda

Pek çok şeyi unutuyoruz yaşamda
Unutmak zorundayız, geleceğimiz pek parlak
   olmayacak yoksa
Sevgi ve nefret üzerimizde dolanıp duruyor sürekli
Böylesine bir felaket açmazdayken hiçbir şey avutmaz
   bizi

Gerçek kahramanlar ya da zavallı sefil varlıklar yok
   bu dünyada
Onur ve kötücüllük yürümez her zaman kol kola
Gerçek iç ve insani değerler yatmaktadır kalbin
   derinliklerinde
Bağışlayıcı kişilerin gözleri dışında kimse giremez o
   duygu haline

Hepimiz biliyoruz ki felaket kışa kanıtlar benzediğini
   kışa
O pamuk beyazı görünüşüyle. Uyaralım! Görmezden
   geliyoruz her şeyi

Mutlu ya da refah içinde yaşıyor olalım gerçek
    anlamda var mı önemi
Eğer kendi özümüzde getiremiyorsak daha parlak
    mevsimleri kıştan sonra.

WE ARE ONE BEING
*Militsa Yeftimijevic Lilic, Serbia*
*Translated by Lazar Macura, Serbia*

Winter will pass, what a wonderful certainty,
life will also pass, we know for sure:
we should not wait – but go toward everything at a
    brisk gait.
„Death will come having your eyes",
Pavese says with certainty
(he does know that),
it must be gentle, beautiful death
like the eyes of love dreamed about by the poet,
better than life that smothers with the rotting stench
of the expired power, of old alliances and glory,
hyenas cannot collect everything
and the certainty of devouring keeps growing

Words bring about chances, miracles, effectuation,
they are echoes of the Soul, the signs of doom, of
    maturation,
keys of the past joy of pain,
dropped silently into the foundations of the verse –
the very essence of the revived
gilding the crust of the irretrievable
for deciphering of the unconceivable.

And when the earth starts boiling again
because of willingness to calm everything down,
once more will I merge into words

turning my eyes from all that noise,
from who is right and who is homeless,
and humbly will I call on letters
that drag along the trail of light,
and I will follow the poem as my guide,
all people walk toward nowhere,
and the poem fused with the bundle of days
sways behind me, shows me and I have no way out.
It is certain, we were and are one being.

## ЈЕДНО ЈЕСМО
*Милица Јефтмијевић Лилић, Србија*


Проћи ће зима, каква дивна извесност,
И живот ће проћи, сигурно знамо:
Не чекати,  у сусрет свему  кораком брзим!
Доћи ће смрт и имаће твоје очи
Са сигурношћу казује Павезе,
(Он то свакако зна)
То мора бити нежна, лепа смрт
Ко очи драге о којој песник сања,
Боља од живота што дави задахом распадања
Минуле моћи, старих савеза, славе.
Хијене не стижу све да скупе
А извесност прождирања  расте.

Речи дозову прилике, чуда, остварење.
Оне су одзиви душе, знак усуда, зрења.
Кључеви минуле моћи, бола
Спуштаних тихо у темељ стиха –
Сама суштина одживљеног
Што злати кору неповратног
За одгонетку несазнатог.

И кад поново тле ускључа
Од хтења главног да све смири,
Ја ћу се опет у речи слити,
Скренути поглед од све те буке,
Ко је у праву а ко без крова.

И скрушено ћу призвати слова
Што траг светлости за собом вуку
Те песму ко водича следити свог.
Ка беспућу нужно иду сви
А она срасла са свежњем дана
Лелуја за мном  и немам куд,
Извесно, једно јесмо, тад и сад!

# CREEPING FROST
*Mohammad Zahid, Kashmir, India*


Every day the expanse of sunlit sky
is growing shorter, minute by minute;
I've been told, the sun too is growing feeble,
its phosphorescent blinding face
slowly melting into Copperish Red.
someone even told me that doors
get shut even before the sun sinks
into the dark ocean of the night
and children are beckoned home
even before crepuscule spreads its claws
lest someone feels short of breath
when the claws race cross the deep valleys.
Somehow I've got to know
that laughter has grown stale
in the damp corner where it was stealthily
stuffed in the old urn and now
there is no place even where to throw it away
for it may stumble out over the precipice
and whine, while rolling into the deep gorge.
The young ones feel terrified
trying to stay as far as possible, from the corner
where the urn rests.
The wise ones keep repeating their words
faith, firewood, fuel and food.
Do, as you are told,

don't you know,
the winter is coming.

# HOW MANY WINTERS PASSED BY
# SINCE YOU WERE GONE
*Osman Öztürk, Turkey*


How many winters passed by since you were gone
Many pains I had since I was in trouble
Since I made a vow to the unfaithful loves
My soul, you turned to winter and I withered

Should there be no longing in this worried heart
Should nobody know about what I have suffered
Should there be no wound making my heart sink
My soul, you turned to winter and I withered

Before autumn arrives I turned to winter
You didn't hear about my trouble, I was weak
I was done for homesickness and had a sigh
My soul, you turned to winter and killed me

# KAÇ KIŞ GELİP GEÇTİ GİTTİN GİDELİ
*Osman Öztürk, Türkiye*

Kaç kış gelip geçti gittin gideli
Kaç kez vurgun yedim derde düşeli
Vefasız aşklara yemin edeli
Kışa çaldın gönül soldurdun beni

Şu gamlı gönülde hasret olmasa
Çektiğim çileyi kimse duymasa
İçimde sızlayan yaran olmasa
Kışa çaldın gönül dondurdun beni

Sonbahar gelmeden ben kışa çaldım
Duymadın derdimi çaresiz kaldım
Gurbetin kahrından ah çekip yandım
Kışa çaldın gönül, öldürdün beni

# WHERE AM I HEADED…?
*Padmaja Iyengar-Paddy, India*


Winter is coming …
I see my distant
land of dreams
on the horizon

Winter is coming …
In this instant
I see a fog-cover
Eclipse the horizon

Winter is coming …
Portending a bleak future,
With no land, no sky
No water, no hope
Where am I headed
I know not …

Winter is coming …
Our rickety boat chugs on…

# OURS IS NOT TO QUESTION WHY
*Padmaja Iyengar-Paddy, India*


Let a fog cover your thoughts
Don't speak out, don't write
Let only your teeth chatter, not you
Let only your survival matter, not others'

Autumn-like gloom …
To subdue our thoughts
To slow our entire being
To stiffen our bones
And silence all phones

Not for me the light
Not for me any fight
I draw the curtains close
To let nothing in …
I snuggle into I, Me, Myself …

# HIJRA –THE EUNUCH
*Preeta Chandran, India*


I wipe the mist from the window;
a sari-clad hijra presses his face to it,
leaving a tiny stain of lipstick.
I roll down the glass and thrust
a ten-rupee note into his hand;
spare me the endearments or the profanities, please.

He utters a few words of gratitude
but I don't spare him another glance.
I fidget in my seat,
willing the lights to turn green,
and blast off, quick as greased lightning.

I don't wipe the red smudge, and all night,
I wonder about the alteration.
Tikku, Shabnam, Brandon Teena,
float in and out of my sleep
and wakefulness.

I recoil at the reason why
I'd hurried with the ten-rupee note.

I cringe at the vision of
the dingy corners of my mind
and the serpents lurking there,
ready to strike;

I wish I'd been more gracious to him.
In the morning, the rains wipe off the smudge.
But they won't wipe off his scars.


Note: The word "hijra" is a Hindustani (Hindi/Indian) word. It has traditionally been translated into English as "eunuch" and indicates irregularity of the male genitalia.

# I DON'T RECOGNIZE MYSELF ANYMORE
*Ra'ed Anis AL-Jishi, Saudi Arabia*
*Translated by Amira Ramah, Tunisia*


The wind weaves a pearl
made of tears on the seeds of earth
and offers it to the hand of uncertainty

me, I resemble the fragments of sand
there where the buds break
to fill the backstage of the story

the plan isn't perfect
the stammering still hovers above the sand
dreams of desertification and tar scent

cement dries all over my hands
its dreams remain yet
undying

what if water comes out of its shady shelter
up to the crust covering my arms

what if water fills each crack between my idle ribs,
screening me as if I were the nails in the broken
    painting of history
I don't recognize myself anymore

if I don't assume myself
the real traits will be as treacherous
as the Arabian gulf

I don't recognize myself anymore

split in half: one half is crucified on the budding
   thorns of spring;
the other, stammering
a threshold of silence

I don't recognize myself anymore

if water fills me in
where the voice is
perhaps then I could be free

THE TIME
*Šimo Ešić, Bosnia and Herzegovina*


My wife has  put  a clock down
In every room of the house
In the kitchen the bathroom
The living room and hall and bedroom
Every ticking of the seconds
Seems like a blow of a hammer
Counting down step by step
How far away I am  from the grave

None of the clocks
Tells the right time
Each is running relentlessly
Turns sometimes unnoticed
Slower or faster
Kept a secret
The terrible question when it really is
When the bell tolls

She just didn't think about
The balcony
There's no clock
That's why I stay there the longest.
Look at the clouds and roofs
Hear through all the city noise
The distant voice
Of a bird in love

126

I do not think of time
Just feel the warmth on my face
From the sun that will go down
As well relentlessly

## SATOVI U KUĆI
*Šimo Ešić, Bosna i Hercegovina*

Žena mi je u svaku prostoriju
postavila po jedan sat –
U kuhinju, hodnik, kupatilo,
dnevnu i spavaću
sobu.
Sad hod sekundare čujem
kao čekića bat
i brojim, kao korak po korak,
da znam koliko sam bliže
grobu.

Ni jedan od njih ne pokazuje
tačno vrijeme.
Svaki žuri nemilice
ili se osjetno sporije vrti.
Tako ostaje tajna
i sve strašne dileme
kad ću pred lice
smrti.

Samo na balkonu
nije se sjetila da ga okači
i tu se sat
ne nalazi.
Tu se najčešće, najradije
i najduže zadržavam.

Gledam u nebo iznad krovova,
kroz tutanj gradske buke
osluškujem udaljen glas
zaljubljene
ptice.
Vrijeme ne mjerim.
Pratim samo sunce
koje mi grije lice
i neumoljivo brzo
zalazi.

# PREPARING FOR WINTER
*Simon Fletcher, United Kingdom*


It starts in late September
when we say goodbye to the swallows.

We gather the last green tomatoes,
haul in plump marrows for chutney.

We collect wood for kindling,
chop logs and pile them close,

pick late raspberries for jam,
blue-frosted sloes for Christmas gin.

Then, from the woods and fields,
we gather mushrooms for drying,

keep an eye on the barometer,
expect cold winds from the north/ east.

# HEARING VOICES
*Simon Fletcher, United Kingdom*


He thought he was hearing voices;
somebody was babbling about depressions,
bad weather to follow.

A fellow was talking about flare ups
in the Middle East; the Russians were firing shells
from the Caspian Sea. Sea shells?

In Africa, a cocktail party at a president's
palace had been stormed by hungry people.
Hungry for cocktails?

The wildfires and twisters raging in the USA
are just natural for that environment, nothing to fear,
a White House spokesman said.

Then he found he was listening to Radio 4.
He'd nodded off during
The World Tonight.

# EMPTY WORDS
*Supratik Sen, India*


How's it a global village
Where one country's failure
Is another's success? Is it
Not the whole world's shame?

Words, only words
For better or for worse,
Playing the blind blame game!

Ganges is connected to Amazon
Like lungs is to kidney
Dubai is linked to London
Like Surat is to Sidney.

Palestine is connected to Hong Kong
Like heart is to brain
Zimbabwe is linked to Wellington
Like forests is to gardens.

The world, much like all sentient beings,
Has cells, tissues, bones, arteries and veins
You may call them towns and cities,
You may regard them as rivers, oceans,
Seas and mountains.
When you are dumping garbage
Onto the weaker territory

Remember this please,
That you maybe healing your elbows
But you might be hurting your knees.

In between your part
Of the world and mine
Stand lonely borders; selfish, alert,
Only empty words shine!

Empty words cannot lure
As boosters of the Game
When a country's failure becomes
The whole world's shame!

Whatever be our past,
Walls will fall, wars will fail,
Forever, they cannot last.
However scarlet the stage
Might have been
Peace will gain its ground
It's bound to rise and win.

# I DIDN'T SCORE A GOAL
*Utz Rachowski, Germany*
*Translated by Louise E. Stoehr, USA*

I didn't score a goal
on that day
played soccer
and the moon passed
terribly round
above the snow
in the bushes
of Hasenheide Park
the sun
did not want to set

on Valentine's Day

As agreed upon
at a right angle
those in love
passed by

I didn't score a goal
on that day
my heart silently struck
the white ice of fear
and rolled out quietly
your gaze on the horizon
I called for you
with mouth tightly closed

Red as a heart shown the sun
on this lovely day
the moon then lay upon
my shoe
sublimely round

# ICH SCHOSS KEIN TOR
*Utz Rachowski, Germany*


Ich schoss kein Tor
an diesem Tag
spielte Fußball
und der Mond ging
fürchterlich rund
überm Schnee
in den Büschen
der Hasenheide
die Sonne
wollte nicht untergehen

am Valentinstag

Wie verabredet
im rechten Winkel
die sich lieben
gingen vorbei

Ich schoss kein Tor
an diesem Tag
mein Herz traf still
das weiße Eis der Angst
und rollte leise aus
dein Blick am Horizont
ich rief nach dir
mit verschlossenem Mund

Herzrot stand die Sonne
an diesem lieben Tag
der Mond lag nun auf
meinem Schuh
vollendet rund

# THE MOOSE AND THE WOLF
*Uwe Friesel, Germany*

To La Fontaine

The wolf came to Åland, the Moose
Was already there
Both knew well how to swim

Throughout the summer
They met on different islands

The wolf ate young lambs and the Moose
Ate young leaves

In the autumn there was hay and sick deer
And both of them
Fooled the trappers and hunters

But suddenly there came ice and snow and
One could see their traces

The moose ate high-up branches
The wolf found a dead mouse

You walk ahead of me  moose
So I can follow your path
The wolf said in a week voice
The moose felt very sorry until
He saw in a crystal of ice

How the wolf sneaked up from behind
And when it was about to jump
The moose flung it with a backward kick
One hundred meters away onto a tree

Please come and fetch me
The wolf implored

I do not eat meat
Retorted the moose over his left shoulder
And walked away

# DER ELCH UND DER WOLF
*Uwe Friesel, Deutschland*

Für La Fontaine


Der Wolf kam nach Åland, der Elch war schon da.
Beide konnten gut schwimmen.

Den Sommer über trafen sie sich
auf verschiedenen Inseln.

Der Wolf fraß junge Lämmer, der Elch junge Blätter.

Im Herbst gab's Heu und kranke Rehe,
und beide überlisteten
die Jäger und die Fallen.

Doch plötzlich kamen Eis und Schnee.
Man sah ihre Spuren.

Der Elch fraß hohe Zweige,
der Wolf fand eine tote Maus.

Geh du vorweg, Elch:
Ich folge Deinem Trampelpfad,
sagte er mit schwacher Stimme.
Der Elch hatte Mitleid. Doch dann
sah er in einem Eiskristall,
wie der Wolf sich von hinten anschlich,
und als der Wolf schon springen wollte,

schlug er ihn mit den Hinterbeinen
hundert Meter weit in einen Baum.

Hol mich herab!
jammerte der Wolf.

Ich esse kein Fleisch,
rief der Elch über die Schulter
Und ging weiter.

# WINTER
*Yiorgos Chouliaras, Greece*


The naked bodies on the snow
on the feathers of birds
on leaves that had fallen
on frozen veins of water
– everything here shows nothing
was able to resist
when winter came again

but we, sunburned,
in cool vessels of vanity
burning whatever we find
will not see winter
bring an end again
if all is finished
when there is no winter

ΧΕΙΜΏΝΑΣ
*Γιώργος Χουλιάρας, Ελλάδα*


Τα γυμνά σώματα στο χιόνι
πάνω στα πούπουλα πουλιών
σε φύλλα που είχαν πέσει
σε παγωμένες φλέβες νερού
– όλα εδώ δείχνουν τίποτε
δεν μπόρεσε να αντισταθεί
όταν πάλι ήρθε ο χειμώνας

αλλά εμείς ηλιοκαμένοι
σε δροσερά δοχεία δόξας
καίγοντας ό,τι βρούμε
χειμώνα δεν θα δούμε
ένα τέλος πάλι να φέρνει
αν όλα θα έχουν τελειώσει
όταν δεν υπάρχει χειμώνας

# WINTER IS ANNOUNCED
*Zorin Diaconescu, Romania*


Winter is announced
we are constantly warned
play with our interpretations
it is not the cold that gnaws at our will
but the fear of it
I thought and wandered
through the empty streets of the city between ideas
That clash in crossroads
there was a state of emergency
no one was capable to sign a law
don't rush a voice said
the winners have a headache,
they are forced
to write history again
the lesson of silence ends here,
the price of peace is clear to us ...
the exchange rate of words was strongly influenced
Compassion is poison
the eye unceasingly watches

# WINTER IST ANGESAGT
*Zorin Diaconescu, Rumänien*


Winter ist angesagt
wir werden dauernd gewarnt
spielen mit unseren Deutungen
es ist nicht die Kälte, die an unserem Willen nagt
sondern die Furcht davor
dachte ich und wanderte
durch die leeren Straßen der Stadt zwischen Ideen
die in Straßenkreuzungen an einander prallten
es herrschte Ausnahmezustand
niemand war imstande ein Gesetz zu unterschreiben
drängt nicht, erklang eine Stimme
die Sieger haben Kopfschmerzen,
sie sind gezwungen,
die Geschichte erneut zu schreiben
die Lektion vom Schweigen endet hier
der Preis der Ruhe ist uns klar…
der Wechselkurs der Worte wurde stark beeinflusst
Mitgefühl vergiftet
das Auge wacht ohne Unterlass

# BİOGRAPHİES

**Ahmet Özer**. Turkish poet, writer, critic, academician. (Born in 1946/Trabzon). He is writing since 1966. His education is Turkish Literature. He worked as a Turkish literature teacher in various government schools of Turkey. After retirement, he worked as an academician in Bilkent University Literary Faculty for long years. He has more than 50 books of poetry, prose and critic. He has many prestigious poetry awards. He took place in many international poetry anthologies and festivals.

**Ali Al-Hazmi** participated in numerous recitals of poetry inside and outside of Saudi Arabia: International Poetry Festival  Costa Rica 2013, Toledo, Spain 2014, Punta del Este, Uruguay  2015, Madrid. Spain 2016, Havana, Cuba 2016, Medellín, Colombia 2016, Istanbul-Turkey 2016, Roma 2017, Romania 2017. He has published the five books of poetry.

**Annabel Villar**, Poet and cultural activist. Founding member of Liceo Poético de Benidorm; Associate Academic and Honorary Member of North American Academy of Modern Literature; Director of "Azul" Poetry Collection; Director of International Poetry Festival "Benidorm & Costa

Blanca"; Founding member of Contemporary Art Student Academy (Rio de Janeiro, Brazil, Chair N° 6 "Gabriela Mistral")

**Anna Nasiłowska**, born 1958, Polish poet, novelist, professor of literature employed in Institute of Literary Research in Warsaw. Author of History of Polish literature (2019). Since 2017 the President of the Association of Polish Writers, board member of Polish P.E.N.- Club. She is also biographer, heroes of her books were Jean-Paul Sartre and Simone de Beauvoir, Maria Pawlikowska-Jasnorzewska and Yoshiho Umeda and his father Ryochu, two Japanese merited for Poland. She has been also the director of Creative Writing course for students for 10 years.

**Joanna Nasiłowska-Rek** (translator), born 1998, student of Ethnology and cultural anthropology in Warsaw University. Also the treasurer of Artists Association Euforis and producer of vocal courses, concerts and events.

**Anna Würth** is an author and photographic artist. Her poems and short stories have been published in 78 anthologies and by Wachholtz in her book *Aphrodite.Lovestoned*. In 2001 she received the Literary Sponsorship Award of GEDOK. She regularly gives public readings both in Germany and abroad. In her 'Literary Pictures' she combines her poems with her photography. They were exhibited in Hamburg, Denmark and in Paphos, Cyprus.

**Dr John Waterfield** (translator). Doctorate in classics and English literature at Christ Church, Oxford. He worked as a music instructor in the UK and Germany.


**Aristea Papalexandrou** was born in Hamburg in 1970. She has published five books of poetry. She has studied music and Medieval and Modern Greek Literature. She works as an editor. For her last book, *It's Passing Us By*, she has been honored by the Academy of Athens, in December 2017.

**Philip Ramp** (translator), born in Michigan, is a poet and experienced translator who has been living and working in Greece for over thirty five years. He has published numerous volumes of original poetry, and done many translations from the Greek.


**Barbara Pogačnik** (1973, Slovenia), poet, translator and literary critic, graduated from UCL in Belgium and completed her MA at the Sorbonne in Paris and has published four poetry books. Her selected poems appreared in Romanian, in French, in Spanish and in Croatian. Her poetry in translations has partially appeared in 30 languages. She has participated in more than 60 different literary manifestations all over the world. More than 150 authors have appeared in her own translations. She has been a member of several literary juries, she is member of PEN, and is on the board of Slovenian Writers Association.

Jernej Žup*a*nič (1982, Slovenia) is a poet, novelist and translator from and into English, graduate of Philosophy and Comparative Literature at the University of Ljubljana. Županič has also published a book of poetry and a novel in 2018, which had won the Critics' Sieve Award for best book 2018.

**Barry Stevenson** is a poet, teacher and translator, living in Hamburg Germany, who did not realize the validity of the order above until 1991.

**Betül Tarıman** is a Turkısh poet and essayist. She studied History at Hacettepe University. Her first poem appeared in Kıyı magazine in 1992 followed by others. She was the recipient of the Necatigil Poetry Prize in 2005. She currently writes literary ads essays for Cumhuriyet Kitap.

**Burkhard P. Bierschenck**, born 1950, spent a part of his youth in the Middle and the Far East. He studied journalism, history and literature (Master) and visited the famous German Journalist's School in Munich. He speaks and writes in German, English and French.

Apart from his career as Journalist, reaching top positions of Editorial Director and General Manager, he wrote more than 25 books, mostly novels and poetry. His acclaimed poetry became part of school curriculum. He was honored with memberships of  HOMER (Historical writers), SYNDIKAT (Crime writers),  UNION DES POÈTES (France) and the PEN Club.


**Chloe Koutsoubelli** was born in Thessaloniki in 1962. She has studied law. Her first collection of poems was published in 1984. Ever since, she has published another eight collections of poems, two novels  and  two theatrical plays. Poems and short stories of hers were published in most of the literary magazines of her country. Many of her poems were translated in English, French, German, Italian, Spanish and Bulgarian. She shared with Stamatis Polenakis the National Award of Poetry in 2017 for her eighth collection of poems.


**Christine Geweke** is a painter, sculptress and lyricist. She is a member of the Hamburger Autorenvereinigung (Hamburg Writers Association) and heads the art room for lyric, paintings and sculptures. On 8.3.2009 she launched the "Charta der SchriftstellerInnen für die Wahrung des Weltfriedens" (charta of authors for the keeping of the world peace) und starts publishing anthologies with peaceful notions. Published five volumes of poetry.


**Claudia Piccinno** was born in southern Italy in 1970, but moved very young to northern Italy where she currently lives and teaches in a primary school. Her poems are in more than a hundred anthologies, she is a member of the jury in numerous national and international literary awards. She is the Director of the Poetry Word Festival for Europe. She has received awards in important national and international poetry competitions. Her poem "In blu" is reproduced on a majolica stele on the seafront of Santa Caterina di Nardo (Le). She has also written numerous critical essays or prefaces to the books of other poets.


**Cordula Scheel** grew up in an open-minded family. She came early in contact with literature in every form, also the Karl May books of her brother contributed to her passion for reading. People and landscapes of the wartime spent in Mecklenburg, Pomerania, Brandenburg and as a refugee child in Holstein has influenced her life. The experiences can be found in her poems. Studied law and languages, first publications towards the end of her professional life.


**Dalia Staponkutė** is an award winning Lithuanian author. She lives outside Lithuania, in Cyprus, and writes in her mother tongue, Lithuanian. Staponkutė is multilingual and is also a translator of Greek literature and an English speaking scholar of literature and translation. Her latest book, The Third Country: My Little Odyssey has garnered great critical acclaim and two prestigious awards – both Lithuanian literary critics and the reading public elected it Book of the Year in 2016. Staponkutė is a board member of the international Three Seas Writers' and Translators' Council, Rhodes, Greece.


**Domenico Pisana** was born in Modica in 1958. He is the Founding President of the Caffè Letterario Quasimodo, a literary circle, which has been promoting for ten years the cultural, poetical and literary valorization of the Iblean territory.

He has been a journalist since 1985 and is the Director of an online newspaper. He published nine poetry books and six volumes about literary criticism. Domenico Pisana's poetry is a matter of international interest. *Il Giornale Italiano de España* wrote about him; the online London newspaper *L'ItaloEuropeo Independent* interviewed him as the "personality of the month", and the French literary review *La Voce* published his interview with Daniela Cecchini. His poems, articles, and prefaces to books by Italian authors were translated in English, Greek, French, Macedonian, Arab, Spanish, Polish, and Romanian language.


**Dorel Cosma,** Romania, holds a B.A. in Journalism, radio-tv producer, senior editor of several newspapers and magazines, chairman of the I.G.F. World Folklore Union, manager of the Palace of Culture, the most important cultural institution of his hometown. Author of several books published in Romania, Bulgaria, Italy, Greece, Egypt, France, Argentina, Germany, Austria, Spain and the USA


**Elizabeth Kurian 'Mona'** writes/translates poetry in English, Hindi, Urdu, Telugu, Malayalam and Marathi. She has thirteen books including translations to her credit, some of which have been illustrated by Sushil Thapa, a well known artist from Kathmandu, Nepal. Mona is the recipient of a number of literary awards. She has taken early retirement as Manager from the Reserve Bank of India, Mumbai. She is associated with various literary groups and is Secretary of the multilingual Sahitya Sangam International, Hyderabad.
**Emel Koşar** was born in Eskişehir (1981). In 2003, she graduated from Turkish Language and

Literature Department of the Faculty of Arts and Sciences of Mimar Sinan University of Fine Arts. She is currently a faculty member at Turkish Language and Literature Department of the same university. She has published her poetry and essays on Turkish literature in various literary magazines. She published her research and review books, scientific and literary works she edited, and 5 poetry collections.

**Yasemin Üşümüş** (translator), was born in İstanbul in 1995. She graduated from Mimar Sinan Fine Arts University with a degree. In 2018, she won her masters degree about Turkish language. She got first place in story writing competition named "Hişt Hişt, Genç Sait Faik."


**Emina Čabaravdić-Kamber** is a poetess, painter and a teacher of exile literature and art, born in Kakanj, Bosnia-Herzegovina and living in Hamburg, Germany since 1968. She is deputy chairwoman of the German Writers Union (VS) in Hamburg and a member of the German Exile PEN. In 1988, she established the international literature club „La Bohemina". She has published books in different languages and received various literary awards. In 1996 Emina Č. Kamber was awarded the Medal of the Order of Merit of the Federal Republic of Germany for her literary work on peace and the ending of the war in Bosnia and Herzegovina.

**Ester Cecere** is author of five poetry books. She has received awards in important national and international poetry competitions and published, by invitation, both in numerous anthologies by various authors and prizes anthologies.


**Fethi Sassi.** Born on the 1. of June in 1962 in Nabul (Tunisia). Writer of prose, poetry, short poems and haiku. Translator of all his poems into English and for many international poets.
Many several translated books published with anthologies.


**Gino Leineweber** was born 1944 in Hamburg/Germany. Since 1998 active as a writer. From 2003 to 2008 he was editor/editor in chief of the Buddhist Monthly Magazine (Buddhistische Monatsblätter).
2003 to 2015 Chairman of the Writers Association Hamburg (Hamburger Autorenvereinigung). Since then Honorary Chairman President of the Three Seas Writers' and Translators' Council (TSWTC) based in Rhodes, Greece from 2013 to 2020. Member in PEN-Centre German-Speaking Writers Abroad (former German Exile-PEN).

He has published novels, short stories, travel books, biographies and poetry. For the latter he has been awarded with international literature prizes.


**Hilal Karahan.** Turkish poetess, writer, translator, and medical doctor (B.1977, Gaziantep/Turkey). She has been writing since 2000. She has 6 poem, 3 prose books and many selected poetry books published in different languages. She has joined to many international collective books, bilingual poetry almanacs. Since she is intercontinental director of World Festival of Poetry (WFP) organization, she is in organization committee of many international poetry festivals. She is recently a member of Turkish PEN, Turkish Authors Association and Turkish Language Society. She is General Secretary of Writers Capital Foundation (WCP) and Turkish Ambassodor of World Institute of Peace (WIP) which are linked to UNESCO. Since 2006, she organizes International Feminİstanbul Woman Poetry Festival every year. She has many national and international poetry awards.


**Holly Iglesias'** work includes three poetry collections and a critical work, Boxing Inside the Box. She has been awarded fellowships by the National Endowment for the Arts, the North Carolina Arts Council, and the Massachusetts

Cultural Council, and teaches at the University of Miami.


**Jenny Lkhagvasuren** works as an English translator and book publisher in Mongolia. She started writing poems in 2013 and her first book of poetry has been published both Mongolian and English. Some of her poems have been published in the Illinois State in USA, Turkey, Italy, Albany, Germany and India in poetry anthologies.
She has translated several books from English to Mongolia and published in Mongolia and aims to write prose besides poems and introduce Mongolian literature to the world.


**Juan C. Tajes,** Uruguay, 1946. Poet and multidisciplinary artist. He has lived in Holland since 1971. He writes poetry, stage plays, narratives and essays. He is organizing cultural events and gives lectures on different subjects. He has literary work published and translated in different countries and participated in international literary festivals. Collaborates with literary magazines in the Nethterlands, Argentina, Brazil and Mexico. He is professor of interpretation for singers at the WMDC Rotterdam Conservatory and teacher of Oratory Art at the University of Political Sciences of Paris.

**Julio Pavanetti.** President of the Int'l Poets Association 'Liceo Poético de Benidorm'. Director of the Int'l Poetry Festival "FIPBECO", Spain. Director of the Poetry Collection "Azul" of Enkuadres Publishers. Spain. Member of the "Association of Spanish Writers and Artists", the "Spanish Collegiate Association of Writers" and the "World Poetry Movement". He has published 13 books. He has been included in more than 60 international anthologies. He has received several awards and recognitions both for his poetry as for his cultural work. He has participated in many international poetry festivals. His poems have been translated into 20 languages.

**K. Pankajam** is a poet/novelist with 19 published books, including 11 books of poems and one translated into French. Her articles, poems, book reviews/papers have been widely published/anthologized. Her poetry has been discussed in detail in the book 'Femininity-Poetic Endeavours' and also in the book 'History of Contemporary Indian English Poetry' under 50 women poets from India. She is the recipient of Oriental Poetry Award 2016, one of the recipients of Ravindranath Tagore Award for Poetry International 2017 and 2018, Bharat award for short stories international 2017, 2018 and 2019, Shree Atal

Behari Vajpayee Award 2019 and Rock Pebbles National Literary Award 2019.

**Liana Sakelliou,** widely anthologized and translated poet, university professor, translator, and literary critic with eighteen books, was awarded two U.S. Fulbright Fellowships, several British Council fellowships, the Marie Curie Intra-European Fellowship, the Stanley J. Seeger Visiting Research Fellowship at Princeton University, and residencies at West Dean College, the University of Sussex, and at the Casa d' Escrita, the University of Coimbra. In 2018 she served as President of the European Jury, while in 2019 as President of the Greek Jury for the EUPL.

**Lily Exarchopoulou** is a writer, critic and translator. She has published three novels, two poetry books, one reader for Greek as a Second Language and her short stories can be found in several anthologies. Her first novel was turned into a play and was staged in Athens. She has worked as a teacher of Literature in Middle and Higher Education and as a cultural editor in newspapers and magazines. Her latest poetry collection (Melani, Dec 2018) has the intriguing title "Clandestine Rage".

**Magie Fauré-Vidot Vijay-Kumar**, from the Seychelles authored seven poetry collections and writes for various international high level magazines. Attended on diverse international literary conferences. She is the Regional Director for South East Africa and Central Asia. She holds the Sey. Govt Award in Literature from 2017 to 2019.

**Maja Herman-Sekulić** (aka Maya Herman) is a multi awarded internationally published Serbian/American author of 19 books published in various languages from English, German, French to Turkish, Mongolian and Malay. She is an acclaimed poet, popular novelist, distinguished essayist, bilingual scholar, and a major translator. A double Fulbrighter, she is also a Princeton Ph.D. in Comparative Literature who taught at prestigious Ivy League universities. She is was recently honored as the Global Poetry Icon, Galaxy Ambassador of World Literature and Good Will, a Style Icon of Serbia and a recepient of the first Serbian Oscar. Born in Belgrade, Maja spent last decade of the last century in the Far East and now shares her time between New York and Belgrade.

**Mallika Chari**, a poet and an artist loves to give colors and shape to her poetry. Her poetry collection Lively Words bears testimony to this wherein each of her poem is represented by her paintings. Her poems have found places in online haiku and haiga journals and poetry anthologies.


**Maren Schönfeld**, poetess and journalist. She has four poetry books and two non-fiction books published so far. In 2017 she received the Poetry Award from the Hamburg Writers' Association (Hamburger Autorenvereinigung).


**Marian Eikelhof** is a poetess, who works in her daily life as a psychologist. Her work inspires her to write about the emotional aspects of life. Not only she describes feelings of love, intimacy and desire, but also she reflects about states of profound sadness and feelings of emptiness. On the whole she criticizes dehumanization and an ongoing process of alienation in human relationships. Marian's poetry book a zero hour contract with life has been translated from Dutch into English and Turkish. Furthermore it is important to state that Marian is an activist for peace and committed to make the world a better place for children.

**Mawar Marzuki** is a poetess, writer, song lyricist, and and a lecturer in the English Department in Penang Institute of Teacher Training and Vice President of Penang Literature Circle and Penang

Malay Heritage Association. She has been invited and participated in different international poetry events apart from others in Mongolia, Istanbul Argentina and South East Asia. Her work was translated and published in Romania, India, Turkey, USA, Germany while her own poetry anthologies were published bilingually.


**Mesut Şenol.** Poet, translator, academician, and journalist. Published poetry collections, and many of his poetry and literary translations appeared in many national and foreign literary publications and anthologies. Attended many national and international literary events. Received numerous literary awards in the country and abroad. A member of many literary organizations. He is currently sitting on the Executive Board of the Three Seas Writers and Translators Council. He teaches at the Translation and Interpreting Studies Department of Yeditepe University, and Communications at the Communications Department of Bahçeşehir University in Istanbul.


**Militsa Yeftimijevic Lilic** is a famous Serbian poetess, writer, critic. Her poems are published in many anthologies and she has many literary awards of national and international importance. She published 26 books. Translated into more than 28 languages as for example in Russian, English, Italian, German, French, Hungarian, Macedonian, Turkish, Swedish, Polish and Arabic. She used to be the vice president of the Association of Writers of Serbia. Lives in Belgrade.

**Mohammad Zahid.** The Pheromone Trail (2013), published by Cyberwit India is the debut award-winning poetry collection by Mohammad Zahid. His poetry has appeared in various anthologies and journals. He has presented his poetry in a few international poetry festivals in India, Hyderabad Literary Festival, Guntur International Poetry Festival, International Multilingual Poets Meet Vijayawada and Pulara 9 Malaysia. He is also a translation editor for Muse India and Lakeview International Journal of Literature and Arts.

**Osman Öztürk** was born in a Black Sea regional province called Giresun. He served for long years at various departments of the Directorate General of the Security of the Turkish Interior Ministry holding high level positions. He also worked at the Turkish embassies in the Washington D.C. and Paris. In 2007 he published five poetry collections and his poetry books were published in a number of countries. His poetry was translated many languages. His poetry collections eflect through his lines with great lucidity, the sincerity of the Turkish folk culture by providing the poet's expressions related to love, loneliness, joy and sorrow, that are all of humane situations to the readers in their mother tongues.

**Padmaja Iyengar-Paddy's** maiden poetry collection 'P-En-Chants' has been recognized as a Unique Record of Excellence by the India Book of Records. She has compiled and edited six international multilingual poetry anthologies, one of women poets 'WWW – Women, Wit & Wisdom' and the others, Amaravati Poetic Prism 2015 to 2019. The 2016, 2017 & 2018 (1111 poems in 107 languages) editions have all been recognized by the renowned Limca Book of Records as "Poetry Anthology in Most Languages". Paddy is a recipient of many awards and a regular invitee to prestigious national and international poetry and literary events.

**Preeta Chandran** is a writer and poet, and the author of the books, 'The Painted Verse' and 'The Portrait of a Verse'. She has been featured in International and Indian anthologies by leading organizations and journals. She has won awards from literary journal Muse India and in the Hindustan Times Brunch Haiku contests. She was formerly an Assistant Vice President with Genpact and is currently CEO at eWandzDigital Services, a digital media firm. She is a Bachelor of Sciences (Honours) in Chemistry, an MBA, and is pursuing a PhD in Management.

**Ra'ed Anis Al-Jishi** is a poet, translator from Saudi Arabia. He has an honorary fellowship in writing from Iowa University, USA. A member of advisory committee of exquisite Teacher training plan of national Changua University of Education-Taiwan. He has been published one novel, ten volumes of poems. A lot of his poems were translated into many languages.

**Amira Rammah** (translator) received a BA in English Language and Literature and pursued an MA in Cross Cultural Studies both from Institut Supérieur des Langues de Tunis (University of Carthage). In 2014, she was selected to participate in the Fulbright Program as a Foreign Language Teaching Assistant of the Arabic language at the University of Iowa. She holds an MFA in literary translation from the University of Iowa. She translates from Arabic and French

**Šimo Ešić** is an author of poems, stories, dramas and radio plays for children. He was born in 1954 in Breze near Tuzla (Bosnia and Herzegovina). He studied Slavonic, then worked as a journalist at Radio Tuzla and Radio Sarajevo and as an editor at the publishing house Univerzal. Since 1990 he has been a freelancer and is the founder and owner of the publishing house Bosanska riječ - The Bosnian Word in Tuzla and Wuppertal.


**Simon Fletcher** lives in the countryside in Shropshire, England, and is widely published. He's performed across Britain and in Pakistan, Norway and Germany. He is manager of Offa's Press and runs poetry writing workshops in green spaces/places. He's read his work on BBC Radio Shropshire and the BBC Asian Network. He runs monthly live literature events in Wolverhampton and Ironbridge, Telford. He also tutors for the Workers' Educational Association. Author of four poetry collections, his most recent, Close to Home, was published by Headland, 2015.


**Supratik Sen** is a blogger. He writes poems, fiction, non-fiction in English, Bangla and in French. His poems have been published in many national and international anthologies.


**Utz Rachowski**, born 1954 in Saxony (Germany), was a former political prisoner in East Germany and was sentenced to 27 months in jail because of five of his poems. He has published 14 books of stories, essays and poetry. Most recently, he received the

2007 Reiner Kunze-Prize and the 2008 Hermann-Hesse-Stipendium. 2013; he was nominated for Pushcart Prize in the US. 2014; Nikolaus-Lenau-Prize. 2017; and received the Prose-Prize from the Society for Contemporary American Literature in German.

**Louise E. Stoehr** (translator), born 1956 in Los Angeles, California, is Associate Professor of German at Stephen F. Austin State University in Nacogdoches, Texas. She completed her B.A. and M.A. in German and Linguistics at Occidental College, and received her doctorate in Germanic Studies from the University of Texas in Austin.


**Uwe Friesel**, after years in Italy and Sweden today lives in Germany. Poet, author and translator. 1991 - 1994 first President of the united German Writers Association after the fall of the Berlin Wall. Co-founder of the international UNESCO-Lit-Centers in Visby and Rhodes. Rewards: Villa Massimo in Rome, Writer in residence in Hamburg and Berlin. German Literature Fonds. Member of PEN.


**Yiorgos Chouliaras** is a Greek poet, essayist, and prose writer, whose work in translation has been published in major English-language periodicals and anthologies as well as in other languages, including Bulgarian, Croatian, French, Japanese, Lithuanian, and Turkish. A recipient of an Academy of Athens award for his work in its entirety, he was a co-founder of influential literary reviews and has been elected president of the Hellenic Authors' Society.


**Zorin Diaconescu**, graduate of the English Language Department of the Faculty of Letters, Babes-Bolyai University, Cluj, Romania. Building a bridge between Romanian and English – a job for a lifetime. Occasionally he writes poetry. He also published a documentary book about the year 1989, writes in and translates into / from: Romanian, German and English.